FARMING THE LAND

Written by Charis Mather

Library of Congress Control Number:
The Library of Congress Control Number is available on the Library of Congress website.

ISBN
979-8-89359-424-9 (library bound)
979-8-89359-444-7 (paperback)
979-8-89359-483-6 (epub)
979-8-89359-464-5 (hosted ebook)

Printed in the United States of America
Mankato, MN
012026

sales@northstareditions.com
888-417-0195

Written by:
Charis Mather

Edited by:
Noah Leatherland

Designed by:
Ker Ker Lee

Image Credits – Images courtesy of Shutterstock.com, unless otherwise stated.

Cover & Recurring – Ysami, Belozer, PCPartStudio, yusufdemirci, Tatiana Vizir, Alyona, Anatolir, Hybrid_Graphics. 4–5 – Minerva Studio, maxim ibragimov. 6–7 – Maya Kruchankova, Longfin Media, Ganna Zelinska, Axl4Real, Mariusz S. Jurgielewicz. 8–9 – oticki, Flystock, Chatrawee Wiratgasem, Zoom Team. 10–11 – Valentin Valkov, Thongsuk7824. 12–13 – Josep Curto, simplystocker, EliaLady. 14–15 – Anatoliy Kosolapov, Deyana Stefanova Robova, Anatoliy Kosolapov, Vereshchagin Dmitry, Photobac. 16–17 –Bule Sky Studio, sima, John Theodor, Juver. 18–19 – Diez10l, Alchemist from India. 20–21 – maxbelchenko, encierro. 22–23 – WESTOCK PRODUCTIONS, Ronnachai Palas.

CONTENTS

Words that look like this can be found in the glossary on page 24.

FARMING IS FASCINATING

Farming is one of the most important jobs in the world. There are many things that farmers need to know to do their jobs well.

Some farmers spend thousands of hours working the land. Farming the land is much more than dropping a seed in the soil and waiting. Let's find out what it really takes.

TYPES OF CROPS

Any plant that is grown for a certain use is called a crop. There are many different kinds of crops.

Food Crops

The most popular food crops are grains, such as wheat, rice, and corn.

Feed Crops

Feed crops, such as hay, are grown for animals to eat.

Fiber Crops

Fiber crops are used for making clothing and paper.

Ornamental Crops

Ornamental crops are plants used for decoration.

Oil Crops

Oil crops can be used for making oil. Oil crops include sunflowers and peanuts.

Industrial Crops

Industrial crops help make useful non-food items.

FARMLAND FACTS

Different kinds of plants have different needs. Not all crops are grown the same way.

Fields

Many crops are grown in rows on large, flat areas of land called fields.

Some fields have hoop houses for keeping plants warm and protected.

Paddies

Paddies are flooded areas of land. They are used to grow crops that need lots of water, such as rice.

Paddies that are layered like steps are called terraces.

Orchards

Orchards are areas of land used for growing fruit or nut trees.

A YEAR ON A FARM

Farmers need to do many different things to make sure they have the best crops at the end of the year. Here are just a few of the jobs they do:

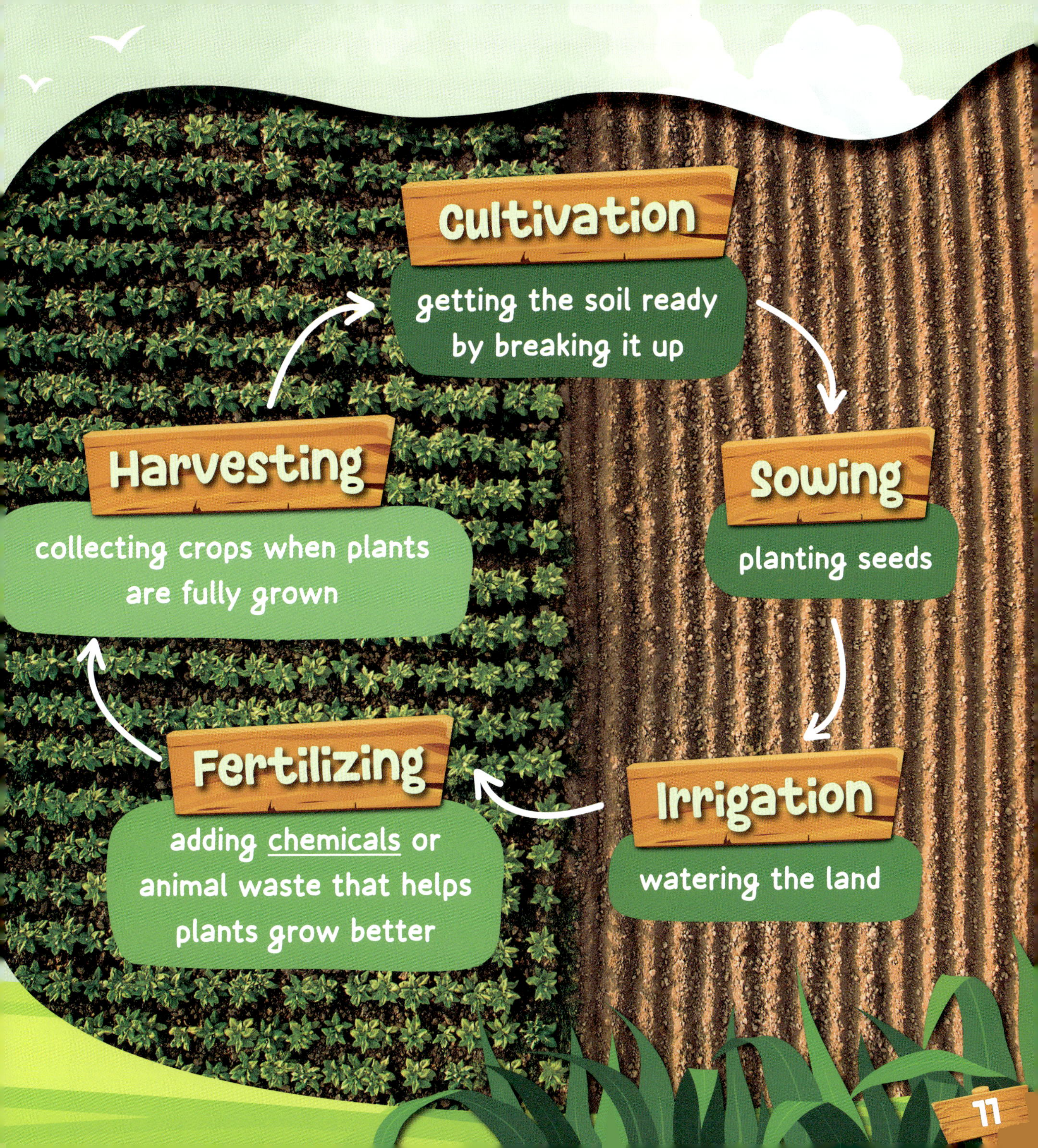

Cultivation

getting the soil ready by breaking it up

Sowing

planting seeds

Irrigation

watering the land

Fertilizing

adding chemicals or animal waste that helps plants grow better

Harvesting

collecting crops when plants are fully grown

ESSENTIAL EQUIPMENT

On big modern farms, equipment is used to make farming quicker and easier. The tractor is the farmer's most important tool. It can attach to other pieces of farm equipment to do different jobs.

Farmers use tractors to mark their fields. They drive along the same lines every time they go through the field. That way, they don't drive over any crops.

Tractor attachments can do all sorts of jobs.

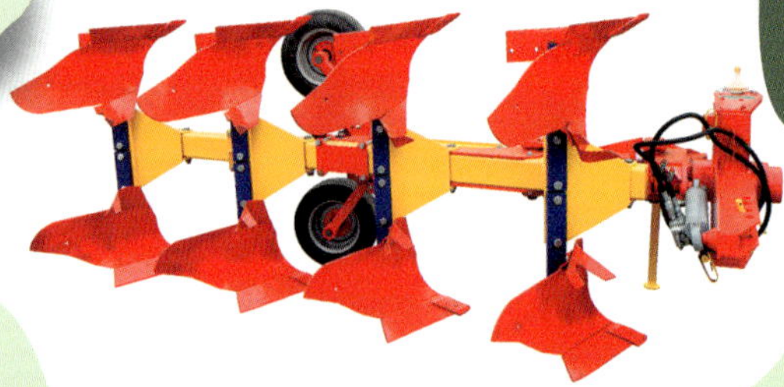

Plows turn over and break apart soil.

Harrows smooth soil.

Sprayers spread water and chemicals over large areas.

Seeders drop seeds in the right amounts.

Trailers move seeds, crops, and other farm equipment.

Balers package hay into bundles.

Some farmers also use combines. These cut down, harvest, and thresh crops when they are ready.

WEATHER, WEEDS, AND OTHER WORRIES

The weather is very important to farmers. If it rains too much or not enough, plants will not grow properly. Farmers will have fewer crops, or none at all.

A DRIED-UP RICE PADDY

A FLOODED CORN FIELD

Weeds also cause farmers trouble. They can take over farmland. More weeds lead to fewer crops.

Insects can eat up fields. Disease can spread through crops quickly. Ruined crops can't be used for food.

FASCINATING FARMING TECHNIQUES

Farmers use many different techniques to help their crops grow year after year.

Irrigation brings water to crops. Pipes, sprinklers, or canals can be used. Irrigation keeps crops watered even when there is no rain.

Over time, crops use up nutrients in the soil. So, many farmers rotate their crops. Crop rotation involves swapping the type of crop in an area. This balances the nutrients that the plants use.

Crop rotation also helps with insect and disease problems.

LOOKING AFTER THE LAND

Some farming practices are not good for the environment. Farmers must be careful. They should farm in a way that looks after the land as well as the crops.

Some farms use chemicals to get rid of insects. However, chemicals can be harmful to other living things, including humans. They can pollute the farmland for a long time.

Organic farms do not use nvironmentally harmful chemicals.

REWARDING WORK

Some farms are massive and modern. Others are small and traditional. All farmers work very hard all year round.

There's a lot farmers need to know to do their jobs. At harvest time, farmers get to enjoy the rewards of their efforts. A good harvest makes it all worthwhile.

GLOSSARY

chemicals substances that can be added to a material to change something about it

environment the natural world

grains small fruits or seeds of some plants, such as wheat and rice

harvest to gather crops

modern to do with recent or present times

nutrients natural substances that plants and animals need to grow and stay healthy

pollute to introduce something harmful or poisonous to an area

thresh to separate the seed from the rest of a grain plant

traditional to do with beliefs, customs, or ways of behaving that have been around for a long time

INDEX